# AI Financial Analysis, Forecasting & Tax Planning

## How Businesses Predict and Control Their Tax Burden

*By Joe Correa*

Published by Live Stronger Faster



This book is for educational and informational purposes only. The author and publisher are not engaged in rendering legal, financial, tax, or other professional advice. Readers should consult a qualified professional before making any financial decisions.

First Edition

# Table of Contents

# Introduction

The most powerful businesses in the modern economy do not simply earn profits—they predict them, shape them, and strategically time them to minimize taxes and maximize retained capital, and in the age of artificial intelligence this ability has been elevated from an elite corporate advantage to a tool available to every entrepreneur, investor, and company that is willing to adopt intelligent systems for financial analysis and forecasting, because taxes are not something that should surprise you at the end of the year but something that should be engineered month by month, decision by decision, and AI now allows businesses to simulate the financial future before it happens, identifying how revenue growth, expense timing, payroll changes, asset purchases, depreciation schedules, inventory decisions, financing structures, and international activity will influence taxable income, cash flow, and long-term wealth, transforming tax planning from guesswork into a science of probability-driven optimization.

Traditional accounting looks backward, recording what already happened and preparing reports that explain the past, but AI-driven financial analysis looks forward, constantly calculating thousands of possible outcomes based on real-time data streams from sales systems, payroll platforms, bank accounts, inventory management, marketing campaigns, and operational dashboards, enabling businesses to see not just what they earned last quarter but what they are likely to earn in three months, six months, or two years and exactly how that income will be taxed under current law, proposed law, and multiple planning scenarios, allowing owners to make smarter decisions today that legally reduce tax exposure tomorrow, and this shift from reactive accounting to predictive tax engineering is one of the greatest wealth-building breakthroughs of the AI era.

For decades, only the largest corporations could afford advanced financial modeling teams that could project taxable income, run tax simulations, and optimize capital structure across entities and jurisdictions, but artificial intelligence has democratized this power by allowing even small businesses and solo entrepreneurs to run sophisticated forecasting models that analyze revenue volatility, expense ratios, payroll growth, depreciation schedules, tax brackets, credits, and deductions, instantly showing how different strategies will impact after-tax profit, cash flow stability, and long-term business valuation, which means that instead of waiting until tax season to find out what you owe, you can now see your tax future in advance and take deliberate actions to control it.

At the heart of AI financial forecasting is the ability to continuously model scenarios, because taxes are not determined by a single number called profit but by a dynamic system of timing, classification, jurisdiction, and structure, and AI excels at identifying how small changes—such as hiring one more employee, purchasing equipment earlier, switching vendors, accelerating marketing spend, or restructuring compensation—can dramatically alter taxable income, payroll tax obligations, sales tax exposure, and credit eligibility, allowing business owners to optimize not only how much they earn but how much of that income they are allowed to keep, which is the true definition of financial intelligence in the modern economy.

This book will show you how AI systems ingest financial data and translate it into tax-aware forecasts that allow you to operate your business like a professional investment fund, where every major decision is evaluated not only for its revenue impact but also for its tax impact, and where capital is deployed in a way that strategically converts taxable income into deductible expenses, depreciable assets, and long-term equity, all while maintaining compliance and audit-ready documentation, giving you the power to grow faster with less friction and more retained earnings.

One of the greatest mistakes businesses make is assuming that tax planning is something that happens once a year, but in reality the tax code is a year-long game of timing and classification, and AI transforms this into a living, breathing system that continuously adjusts projections as new data flows in, allowing you to know in real time whether you are on track for a large tax bill, a refund, or an opportunity to reinvest profits into tax-advantaged strategies, and this ongoing feedback loop is what separates companies that are always scrambling to pay taxes from those that use taxes as a strategic lever for growth.

AI-powered financial forecasting also allows businesses to model risk, because not all revenue is equal and not all expenses create the same tax outcome, and modern AI systems can analyze volatility, customer concentration, seasonal patterns, debt levels, and operational costs to determine how stable your future income is and how resilient your tax position will be under different economic conditions, which is especially critical for companies that operate across multiple states, countries, or digital platforms, where tax exposure can shift rapidly based on changing regulations and business activity.

Another major advantage of AI-driven financial analysis is its ability to simulate the long-term effects of today's decisions, such as how buying versus leasing equipment will impact depreciation and taxable income over five years, how hiring contractors versus employees changes payroll taxes and deductions, how inventory strategy affects cost of goods sold, and how different entity structures influence retained earnings and reinvestment potential, giving business owners the clarity they need to make decisions that build wealth instead of accidentally creating future tax burdens.

This book will also explore how AI integrates tax planning directly into cash flow management, because paying taxes is not just about how much you owe but when you owe it, and AI systems can forecast estimated tax payments, payroll deposits, sales tax remittances, and corporate filings so that businesses never experience liquidity shocks, allowing them to invest, hire, and expand with confidence, knowing that their tax obligations have already been accounted for in their financial strategy.

As governments around the world move toward real-time reporting, digital tax accounts, and automated compliance, AI-driven forecasting will become even more essential, because the future of taxation will not allow businesses to hide mistakes or fix errors months later, and instead will require continuous accuracy and predictive alignment between financial activity and tax obligations, making AI not just a competitive advantage but a necessity for survival in the digital tax economy.

By the end of this book, you will understand how to use artificial intelligence to transform raw financial data into a predictive tax-planning engine that allows you to anticipate liabilities, identify opportunities, and build strategies that convert income into lasting wealth, and you will see how businesses that master AI financial forecasting are able to scale faster, retain more profit, and operate with a level of clarity and control that was once reserved only for global corporations with massive finance departments.

AI does not replace accountants or tax professionals; it empowers them and the business owners they serve by providing a continuously updated financial and tax intelligence system that highlights risks, opportunities, and optimization pathways before they become costly surprises, creating a future where businesses no longer fear tax season but instead treat it as a strategic checkpoint in a larger wealth-building plan.

This book is your gateway into that future, where financial forecasting, tax planning, and artificial intelligence merge into a single system of intelligent decision-making that gives you control over not only what you earn but what you keep, how you grow, and how you protect the wealth you create, setting the foundation for the advanced strategies explored in the final volume of this series as we move toward a fully automated, AI-powered tax economy.

*Chapter 1*

# The AI Financial Engine: Turning Data Into Predictive Tax Intelligence

Modern businesses no longer succeed by simply recording what happened; they succeed by predicting what will happen, and artificial intelligence has become the engine that makes this possible by transforming streams of financial data into forward-looking insight that allows companies to engineer their tax outcomes rather than react to them, because every sale, every expense, every payroll run, and every capital purchase creates a ripple effect that flows through the tax system, and AI is uniquely capable of tracing those ripples through time, showing how today's decisions will shape tomorrow's liabilities and opportunities in ways that human analysis alone could never compute with enough speed, depth, or accuracy to matter in a fast-moving business environment.

At the core of this transformation is the AI financial model, which continuously absorbs data from accounting software, point-of-sale systems, payroll platforms, banks, inventory tools, marketing dashboards, and even economic indicators, using that information to construct a real-time digital twin of the business that reflects not just its current position but its projected future under thousands of potential scenarios, allowing leaders to see how different revenue levels, cost structures, staffing changes, and investment decisions will affect taxable income, cash flow, and compliance obligations months or even years into the future.

Unlike traditional spreadsheets that rely on static assumptions and manual updates, AI forecasting engines update themselves every time new data enters the system, recalculating profit projections, depreciation schedules, payroll taxes, estimated payments, and credit eligibility in real time, so instead of waiting until the end of a quarter to discover that tax exposure has exploded, businesses can see the problem forming weeks in advance and take corrective action by adjusting spending, accelerating deductions, restructuring compensation, or shifting capital into tax-efficient assets.

One of the most powerful aspects of AI-driven financial analysis is its ability to understand the tax code not as a list of rules but as a complex decision tree where timing, classification, and structure determine outcomes, because when AI sees a new expense it does not merely record it but evaluates whether it is deductible, depreciable, capitalizable, or credit-eligible, and when it sees new revenue it determines how that income will be taxed based on entity type, jurisdiction, and the availability of offsets, creating a living tax strategy that evolves as the business evolves.

This predictive layer is what allows companies to operate with what can be called tax awareness, meaning that every financial action is evaluated not just for its business impact but for its tax impact, so when a company considers hiring, expanding into a new state, launching a new product line, or acquiring equipment, AI can instantly show how that move will affect payroll taxes, sales taxes, income taxes, and compliance requirements, allowing leaders to make informed decisions that maximize after-tax profitability instead of blindly increasing taxable income.

AI also excels at identifying patterns that humans miss, such as seasonal revenue cycles, expense spikes, customer concentration risk, and cash flow volatility, and it uses these patterns to adjust tax forecasts dynamically, ensuring that estimated payments are accurate, reserves are sufficient, and opportunities for deductions and credits are not lost simply because someone failed to notice a trend forming in the data.

In an increasingly global and digital economy, where businesses sell across borders, employ remote workers, and operate on multiple platforms, AI becomes even more critical because tax exposure can shift rapidly as revenue is sourced in different jurisdictions, and intelligent systems can track nexus, withholding, VAT, and reporting obligations in parallel with financial forecasting, allowing companies to expand without stepping into regulatory traps that can destroy profitability.

By integrating financial forecasting with tax planning, AI creates a new operating system for business, one in which profitability, compliance, and growth are no longer competing priorities but interconnected outputs of a single intelligent process that continuously seeks the most efficient path forward, and this is the foundation upon which modern, high-performing, tax-optimized companies are built.

*"The Numbers That Knew the Future"*

When Elena first opened her digital marketing agency, she thought success meant watching the revenue line climb on her accounting dashboard, but after her first profitable year ended with a crushing tax bill that wiped out most of her cash reserves, she realized that earning money and keeping money were two very different games, and it was only when she implemented an AI-powered financial forecasting system that she began to understand how the future of her business was quietly being written by the numbers she was generating every day.

At first, the AI simply organized her data, pulling transactions from her bank, categorizing expenses, and reconciling invoices faster than any bookkeeper ever could, but within weeks it began producing projections that startled her, showing that if her growth continued at its current pace she would owe more in taxes over the next twelve months than she had ever paid before, and worse, that her cash flow would not be sufficient to cover those obligations without slowing down hiring or cutting marketing, which forced her to confront the reality that growth without planning could actually bankrupt her.

The AI did not just warn her of danger, it offered solutions, showing her that by adjusting the timing of equipment purchases, restructuring her compensation, and shifting certain contractors into payroll roles, she could legally reduce her tax exposure while still expanding, and as Elena followed the recommendations, she watched in real time as her projected tax burden dropped and her future cash position stabilized, giving her a sense of control she had never experienced before.

As her business expanded into new states and began serving international clients, the AI adapted, tracking sales tax nexus, withholding obligations, and compliance thresholds automatically, alerting her whenever a new filing requirement emerged, and instead of being blindsided by regulatory complexity, Elena found herself ahead of it, making strategic decisions about where to grow based on after-tax profitability rather than just gross revenue.

The most surreal moment came when the AI predicted a cash crunch six months in advance based on seasonal client churn and rising payroll costs, and because she had that warning early, Elena was able to secure financing, adjust her pricing, and build reserves that allowed her to sail through a period that would have crushed her without preparation, proving that financial intelligence was not about reacting quickly but about seeing the future clearly enough to act calmly.

By the third year, Elena's agency had become a machine of disciplined growth, with every decision evaluated not just for how much it would earn but for how it would be taxed, and she realized that her AI was not just an accounting tool but a strategic partner that continuously shaped her business into its most profitable, resilient, and compliant form.

Looking back, she no longer feared tax season, audits, or expansion, because the numbers were no longer a mystery, and in a world where uncertainty ruins so many entrepreneurs, Elena had gained something priceless: a business that knew its own future and had the intelligence to design it.

*Chapter 2*

# Scenario Modeling: How AI Simulates Your Tax Future

The true power of artificial intelligence in financial and tax planning lies not merely in its ability to calculate what will happen if you stay on your current path, but in its ability to simulate what would happen if you change course, because every business exists inside a web of possibilities where revenue can rise or fall, expenses can expand or contract, laws can shift, and markets can evolve, and AI makes it possible to model these possibilities in advance, turning uncertainty into strategic foresight that allows business owners to choose the most profitable and tax-efficient future rather than being forced to accept whatever outcome happens to occur.

Scenario modeling works by creating thousands of parallel financial universes inside the AI system, each one representing a different version of the business based on varying assumptions such as higher or lower sales, different hiring schedules, new equipment purchases, changes in pricing, geographic expansion, or shifts in tax law, and in each of these simulated worlds the AI calculates taxable income, payroll taxes, sales tax exposure, depreciation schedules, credit eligibility, and cash flow, allowing decision-makers to see not just what is likely to happen but what could happen under a wide range of conditions.

This approach completely transforms how businesses plan, because instead of guessing how a major decision will affect taxes, they can test it before committing, seeing in advance whether hiring five employees versus three will push them into a higher tax bracket, whether purchasing equipment now or later will generate greater depreciation benefits, or whether expanding into a new state will create sales tax and compliance obligations that outweigh the expected revenue, giving them the ability to make moves that are strategically brilliant rather than financially reckless.

AI scenario modeling is also uniquely powerful because it does not rely on single-point forecasts but on probability distributions, meaning it evaluates not only the most likely outcome but also best-case and worst-case scenarios, showing how resilient a company's tax and cash flow position will be if growth exceeds expectations or falls short, and this allows businesses to design strategies that perform well across a wide range of conditions instead of collapsing when reality deviates from the plan.

One of the greatest advantages of this approach is its ability to highlight tax tipping points, which are moments where small changes in income or expenses cause disproportionately large changes in tax liability, such as when a company crosses into a new tax bracket, loses eligibility for a credit, triggers alternative minimum tax exposure, or creates nexus in a new jurisdiction, and by identifying these thresholds in advance, AI allows businesses to structure their growth in ways that avoid unnecessary tax spikes and preserve capital.

Scenario modeling also enables sophisticated timing strategies, because AI can show how shifting revenue recognition, expense payments, asset purchases, and compensation can move taxable income between periods in ways that optimize deductions and credits, allowing businesses to smooth their tax burden over time rather than experiencing painful peaks that strain cash flow and limit reinvestment.

As governments introduce more frequent reporting, real-time compliance, and digital tax systems, scenario modeling becomes even more valuable because it allows businesses to anticipate regulatory changes and adjust their operations before new rules take effect, protecting profitability and compliance in an increasingly automated and transparent tax environment.

Ultimately, AI-driven scenario modeling turns financial planning into a strategic game where businesses can see the full map of possible futures and choose the path that leads to the highest after-tax returns, the strongest cash flow, and the greatest long-term stability, making tax planning not a defensive exercise but a proactive driver of growth and wealth.

*"Choosing Tomorrow"*

When Marcus launched his e-commerce brand, he believed that growth was always good, but after a rapid expansion left him facing unexpected sales tax obligations, payroll taxes, and a massive income tax bill, he realized that the future of his business depended not just on how fast it grew but on how intelligently it evolved, and it was only when he adopted an AI-driven scenario modeling system that he began to see the many possible tomorrows his company could face.

The AI showed him multiple paths, one where he continued to scale aggressively without planning and ended up cash-strapped by taxes, another where he slowed growth too much and lost market share, and a third where he optimized hiring, inventory, and pricing to maximize after-tax profit, and for the first time Marcus could see that success was not a single destination but a choice between different financial realities.

As he adjusted variables inside the system, watching projected tax bills rise and fall with each decision, Marcus learned how small changes could create massive differences in outcome, and by choosing the path that balanced growth with tax efficiency, he transformed what once felt like chaos into a clear and controllable strategy.

Months later, when new sales tax rules threatened to derail his expansion, the AI had already modeled their impact, allowing Marcus to adjust his fulfillment and pricing in advance, and while competitors scrambled to react, his business continued to grow smoothly, protected by foresight.

In the end, Marcus realized that the true gift of AI was not that it predicted the future, but that it allowed him to choose it, and with that power, his company became not just bigger, but smarter, more resilient, and far more profitable.

*Chapter 3*

# From Forecast to Action: Using AI to Execute Tax-Smart Decisions

Artificial intelligence becomes truly transformative for businesses not when it merely predicts the future, but when it actively guides decisions that shape that future, because forecasting without action is just information, while forecasting combined with intelligent execution becomes a powerful engine for profit optimization and tax control, allowing companies to move beyond awareness and into a state where every financial choice is aligned with a deliberate, data-driven strategy to minimize taxes, stabilize cash flow, and accelerate sustainable growth.

AI systems turn forecasts into action by connecting financial projections directly to operational workflows, so when projected taxable income rises above a desired threshold the system can recommend accelerating deductible expenses, shifting compensation structures, increasing retirement contributions, or purchasing qualifying assets, and when cash flow risk appears the system can advise delaying nonessential spending, renegotiating vendor terms, or adjusting pricing, effectively acting as a continuously operating financial advisor that keeps the business on track even as conditions change.

This capability is especially powerful because tax planning is not a single decision but a series of micro-decisions made throughout the year, and AI monitors these in real time, constantly comparing actual results to forecasts and triggering alerts or recommendations when the business drifts away from its optimal tax path, ensuring that opportunities for deductions, credits, and strategic timing are not lost simply because someone forgot to check a report or misunderstood a trend forming in the data.

By integrating forecasting with budgeting, payroll, procurement, and accounting systems, AI creates a closed-loop financial ecosystem where every dollar that enters or leaves the business is evaluated for both its economic and tax impact, allowing leaders to see how operational changes ripple through profitability and compliance, and to choose actions that maximize after-tax returns without sacrificing growth or stability.

One of the most important functions of AI-driven execution is its ability to prioritize decisions, because not all tax strategies are equally valuable at all times, and intelligent systems can rank opportunities based on their projected impact, cost, and risk, helping businesses focus on the actions that will deliver the greatest financial benefit rather than chasing every possible deduction or deferral.

AI also enhances collaboration between business owners, accountants, and tax professionals by providing a shared, real-time model of the company's financial future, allowing advisors to test strategies, validate assumptions, and implement plans with confidence, reducing misunderstandings and improving the quality of strategic guidance.

As digital tax systems become more automated and governments demand greater transparency, AI-driven execution will become essential for maintaining compliance while still optimizing outcomes, because businesses will no longer be able to rely on after-the-fact adjustments and instead must operate in continuous alignment with tax rules, and intelligent systems provide the only scalable way to achieve this without overwhelming human teams.

Ultimately, AI transforms tax planning from a reactive chore into an active management discipline, where businesses continuously steer themselves toward the most profitable and compliant version of their future, turning forecasting into a living strategy that evolves with every transaction and every decision.

*"The Profit Path"*

When Sophia took over her family's manufacturing company, she inherited not just a legacy but a mountain of financial complexity, and although the business was profitable, unpredictable tax bills and cash flow swings made growth feel like a gamble rather than a strategy, until she implemented an AI-driven financial execution system that began turning forecasts into daily guidance for every decision she made.

The AI showed her how planned equipment purchases would reduce taxable income, how adjusting employee bonuses would affect payroll taxes, and how shifting production schedules could smooth cash flow, and as Sophia followed its recommendations, she watched her projected tax burden drop while her actual profits rose, giving her the confidence to invest in new machinery and expand into new markets without fear.

When a sudden surge in orders threatened to push the company into a higher tax bracket, the AI immediately suggested accelerating capital expenditures and increasing retirement contributions for key employees, actions that not only reduced taxes but also strengthened the company's long-term position, and Sophia realized that the system was not just reacting to change but actively shaping a better outcome.

Over time, the business became more predictable, more resilient, and more profitable, because every decision was guided by a clear understanding of its future impact, and Sophia found herself no longer stressed by tax season or economic uncertainty, knowing that her company was always on the most efficient path forward.

Looking back, she understood that the true value of AI was not in the numbers it produced, but in the confidence it gave her to lead, because when you can see the road ahead, you can drive faster, take smarter turns, and reach destinations that once seemed impossible.

*Chapter 4*

# Cash Flow, Timing, and Tax Control: How AI Orchestrates When You Pay and When You Keep

Taxes are not destroyed by strategy; they are shifted through time, and the businesses that master tax optimization are not those that earn the least but those that control when income is recognized, when expenses are incurred, and when obligations are paid, because cash flow timing is the invisible lever that determines whether taxes feel manageable or suffocating, and artificial intelligence has become the first system capable of continuously orchestrating this timing at scale, aligning revenue, expenses, payroll, capital investments, and estimated payments into a coordinated financial rhythm that preserves liquidity while remaining fully compliant.

Traditional tax planning often focuses on totals—total income, total expenses, total tax owed—but AI understands that timing matters just as much as magnitude, because two businesses with identical annual profits can experience wildly different tax outcomes depending on when revenue arrives, when deductions are taken, and when cash leaves the business, and AI-driven cash flow forecasting models these dynamics in real time, showing how monthly, quarterly, and seasonal fluctuations affect taxable income and liquidity, allowing businesses to smooth tax impact rather than being crushed by concentrated obligations.

AI systems continuously project cash inflows and outflows while simultaneously layering tax rules on top of those projections, calculating estimated tax payments, payroll deposits, sales tax remittances, and corporate obligations weeks or months in advance, which allows business owners to plan spending and investment around known obligations instead of reacting to surprise deadlines, transforming taxes from emergencies into scheduled events that are already accounted for in the company's financial plan.

This orchestration becomes especially powerful when AI coordinates timing strategies, such as accelerating deductible expenses into high-income periods, delaying income recognition where legally permitted, optimizing depreciation schedules, and aligning capital expenditures with forecasted tax peaks, ensuring that cash is deployed in ways that reduce taxable income precisely when it matters most, while avoiding actions that would create unnecessary liabilities or compliance risk. AI also plays a critical role in protecting businesses from liquidity shocks, because tax bills rarely arrive alone and often coincide with payroll, inventory purchases, or debt payments, and intelligent systems can identify upcoming congestion points where multiple obligations overlap, recommending adjustments such as deferring nonessential spending, renegotiating vendor terms, or restructuring payment schedules to maintain operational stability.

In businesses with variable revenue—such as e-commerce, real estate, professional services, and seasonal operations—AI-driven cash flow and tax alignment becomes essential, because uneven income can trigger uneven tax burdens, and predictive systems allow companies to reserve cash during strong months to cover future obligations, preventing the feast-or-famine cycle that destroys so many growing enterprises.

As tax authorities move toward real-time reporting and automated collection, the margin for error in timing will shrink, making AI not just an optimization tool but a survival mechanism that ensures businesses remain synchronized with regulatory systems while still operating at peak efficiency, and those that fail to adopt intelligent cash flow orchestration will increasingly find themselves paying more taxes not because they earned more, but because they planned less.

Ultimately, AI transforms cash flow and tax timing into a single, integrated discipline where money moves through the business with intention, foresight, and control, allowing owners to grow confidently, invest strategically, and retain more of what they earn without fear of unexpected tax consequences.

*"The Quarter That Almost Broke Everything"*

Daniel had always believed that cash in the bank meant safety, and for years his construction firm appeared healthy on paper, with steady contracts, growing revenue, and a solid reputation, but beneath the surface the business was drifting toward a crisis he could not see, because while money was coming in, it was leaving faster than he realized, and taxes were silently positioning themselves to strike all at once, waiting for the exact moment when cash flow would be weakest.

The warning came quietly, not as a crisis but as a forecast, when the AI system Daniel reluctantly installed began projecting the next twelve months of cash flow and tax obligations, and what it showed him was terrifying: a single quarter where payroll expansion, equipment purchases, estimated tax payments, and sales tax remittances would collide, creating a cash deficit large enough to force layoffs or emergency financing, and the most alarming part was that nothing about that quarter looked unusual on the surface, because the danger was not in any single decision but in their combined timing.

At first Daniel doubted the projection, convinced that something so catastrophic would have been obvious, but as the AI walked through the numbers—showing when contracts would pay, when materials had to be purchased, when payroll would spike, and when tax deposits would be due—he saw how the problem formed not from mismanagement but from a lack of coordination, where perfectly reasonable decisions stacked on top of each other until they became lethal.

The AI did not panic, and neither did it shame him; instead it offered alternatives, modeling dozens of small adjustments that together reshaped the future, suggesting that equipment purchases be split across quarters to optimize depreciation timing, that certain contracts be invoiced earlier to pull cash forward, that estimated tax payments be recalculated based on updated projections, and that vendor terms be renegotiated to spread cash outflows more evenly, and as Daniel applied each recommendation, he watched the red deficit line slowly fade into a stable, manageable projection.

What stunned him most was how little had to change to avoid disaster, because the AI did not ask him to grow less or work harder, but simply to move the same money through the business at smarter times, and as the quarter approached, instead of bracing for impact, Daniel found himself calm, prepared, and liquid, with taxes paid, payroll covered, and reserves intact. When the quarter finally passed, it felt almost anticlimactic, because what had once been projected as a breaking point became just another phase of growth, and Daniel realized that the greatest threat to his business had not been taxes themselves, but ignorance of timing, because without foresight, even profitable companies can collapse under the weight of obligations that arrive all at once.

In the months that followed, Daniel stopped thinking of taxes as an annual event and began viewing them as a constant current flowing through his business, one that needed to be guided rather than resisted, and with the AI orchestrating cash flow and tax timing in the background, he no longer feared expansion, because he knew that every dollar earned already had a plan for when it would be kept, when it would be paid, and when it would be reinvested.

Years later, when younger contractors asked him how he survived periods that crushed others, Daniel never talked about luck or grit; he talked about visibility, about seeing the future clearly enough to act before it arrived, and he understood that the quarter that almost broke everything had instead taught him the most valuable lesson of his career: profits mean nothing without timing, and timing is power when intelligence controls it.

*Chapter 5*

# Risk, Resilience, and Tax Stability: How AI Stress-Tests Your Financial Future

Taxes are not paid in a vacuum; they are paid inside real economic conditions shaped by volatility, uncertainty, and risk, and the businesses that survive long enough to build lasting wealth are not those that experience the least disruption but those that anticipate disruption early enough to absorb it without collapse, and artificial intelligence has become the most powerful tool ever created for stress-testing a company's financial and tax position against the unpredictable forces of markets, regulation, consumer behavior, and internal growth dynamics.

AI-driven risk modeling goes far beyond traditional contingency planning by continuously analyzing historical patterns, current performance, and external signals to simulate how financial and tax outcomes change under stress, such as revenue drops, customer loss, supply chain interruptions, interest rate shifts, regulatory changes, or unexpected expenses, allowing businesses to see in advance how resilient their cash flow, tax reserves, and compliance position truly are when conditions deteriorate. This capability is critical because taxes often become most dangerous precisely when businesses are under pressure, as declining revenue can coincide with fixed obligations like payroll taxes, estimated payments, debt service, and regulatory filings, creating situations where companies that were profitable on paper suddenly become insolvent in practice, and AI allows leaders to identify these vulnerabilities early by modeling worst-case and near-worst-case scenarios that reveal how quickly liquidity erodes and where intervention is required.

AI stress testing also exposes structural weaknesses in tax strategy, such as overreliance on volatile income streams, poor expense timing, excessive jurisdictional complexity, or insufficient reserves for payroll and sales tax obligations, and by surfacing these issues long before they cause harm, AI gives businesses the opportunity to redesign their operating model in ways that increase stability without sacrificing growth.

Another key advantage of AI risk analysis is its ability to differentiate between temporary shocks and systemic threats, allowing businesses to respond appropriately rather than overreacting to short-term noise or ignoring slow-building dangers, and this clarity enables more precise tax planning decisions, such as whether to conserve cash, accelerate deductions, delay expansion, or invest aggressively during downturns when tax advantages may be greatest. AI also helps businesses prepare for regulatory risk by simulating the impact of tax law changes, enforcement shifts, and reporting requirements, ensuring that companies are not caught off guard by new compliance burdens that can disrupt cash flow or trigger penalties, and as governments increasingly rely on automated systems and real-time data, this predictive awareness becomes essential for maintaining stability.

By integrating stress testing with forecasting and execution, AI creates a resilient financial framework where businesses do not merely survive volatility but adapt to it intelligently, using foresight to maintain compliance, preserve cash, and protect long-term value even when conditions deteriorate.

In this way, AI transforms tax planning from a static exercise into a dynamic risk-management discipline, ensuring that profitability is not only optimized during good times but preserved during difficult ones, allowing businesses to grow with confidence knowing that their financial future has been tested, reinforced, and intelligently protected.

*"The Year the Numbers Turned Against Him"*

When Robert finally admitted that something felt wrong, it was not because revenue had collapsed or clients had vanished, but because despite working harder than ever, his professional services firm felt increasingly fragile, as if a single unexpected event could knock it off balance, and although the books looked acceptable on the surface, there was a quiet tension beneath the numbers that he could not explain until the AI system he reluctantly adopted showed him what his intuition already knew but could not yet prove.

The first report the AI generated was not dramatic, and that was what made it unsettling, because instead of forecasting growth or decline, it simulated stress, showing what would happen if revenue dropped by ten percent, then fifteen, then twenty, and with each reduction the tax obligations did not fall at the same rate, because payroll taxes, estimated payments, and compliance costs remained stubbornly fixed, and by the time the simulation reached a moderate downturn, the firm's cash reserves were gone and penalties had begun to appear, not because of mismanagement, but because the structure of the business was not built to absorb shock.

Robert stared at the projections late into the night, watching scenario after scenario unfold where nothing catastrophic happened at first, but where small disruptions accumulated until the business crossed an invisible threshold beyond which recovery became almost impossible, and what frightened him most was that none of the scenarios required bad decisions or negligence, only ordinary volatility that any business could face.

The AI did not stop at diagnosis; it began suggesting structural changes, showing how diversifying revenue timing, restructuring compensation, building tax reserves, and simplifying jurisdictional exposure could dramatically increase resilience, and as Robert implemented each recommendation, the simulations changed, showing that the same downturns that once destroyed liquidity could now be absorbed with reserves intact and compliance maintained.

Then came the real test, when a major client unexpectedly reduced its contract, sending a ripple through the firm's revenue stream, and while panic spread among Robert's peers, he found himself calm, because the AI had already shown him this future, had already prepared him for it, and had already guided him through the actions that would preserve stability, allowing him to respond decisively rather than emotionally.

As months passed, the downturn deepened, but Robert's firm remained standing, paying taxes on time, maintaining payroll, and even investing selectively while competitors cut back or collapsed, and it was only then that he fully understood the difference between optimism and resilience, because optimism hopes for the best, while resilience prepares for the worst without surrendering ambition.

By the time conditions improved, Robert's firm emerged stronger, leaner, and more strategically designed than before, not because it had avoided hardship, but because it had faced it with foresight, and when he reviewed the year in hindsight, he realized that the moment that saved everything was not when the crisis hit, but when the numbers first turned against him inside the simulation, quietly offering him the chance to change the future before it arrived.

From that year on, Robert no longer asked whether his business was profitable; he asked whether it was resilient, because he had learned that wealth is not measured by how much you earn in good times, but by how well you protect what you earn when conditions turn against you, and in that understanding, guided by intelligent forecasting, he finally felt secure.

*Chapter 6*

# Scaling Without Penalty: How AI Aligns Growth With Tax Efficiency

Growth is often celebrated as the ultimate marker of success, yet for many businesses it becomes the very force that destroys profitability, because scaling without foresight can magnify tax exposure faster than revenue, creating a situation where companies work harder, earn more, and paradoxically keep less, and artificial intelligence has emerged as the only system capable of aligning expansion with tax efficiency in a way that allows businesses to scale deliberately, sustainably, and intelligently without triggering unnecessary penalties, compliance failures, or cash flow strain.

As businesses grow, complexity multiplies, because more revenue means higher estimated payments, more employees mean increased payroll taxes and filings, more locations mean additional sales tax and nexus exposure, and more assets mean complicated depreciation schedules, and AI is uniquely suited to manage this complexity because it does not rely on static rules but continuously recalculates how each incremental step of growth affects the entire tax and financial ecosystem of the company. AI-driven scaling analysis allows businesses to forecast not just whether growth is possible, but whether it is optimal, modeling how different rates of expansion affect after-tax profit, liquidity, and long-term valuation, and this insight is critical because the fastest-growing path is rarely the most profitable one once taxes, compliance costs, and operational risk are accounted for, and intelligent systems help leaders choose growth strategies that maximize retained earnings rather than headline revenue.

One of the most important contributions of AI in scaling is its ability to identify growth friction points, which are moments where expansion creates disproportionate tax or compliance burden, such as crossing employee thresholds that trigger new regulations, entering jurisdictions that impose complex reporting requirements, or reaching income levels that reduce eligibility for credits and incentives, and by identifying these points in advance, AI allows businesses to plan around them rather than being blindsided.

AI also enables smarter reinvestment strategies by showing how profits can be redirected into tax-advantaged uses such as equipment purchases, research and development, employee benefits, and retirement contributions, allowing businesses to convert taxable income into long-term value while continuing to grow, and this reinvestment loop becomes the engine that fuels sustainable expansion without eroding cash reserves. As organizations scale across states or borders, AI plays a critical role in managing multi-jurisdictional tax exposure by tracking nexus, withholding, transfer pricing considerations, and reporting obligations in parallel with growth forecasts, ensuring that expansion does not inadvertently create regulatory liabilities that outweigh its benefits.

Ultimately, AI transforms scaling from a risky leap into a calculated progression, where each stage of growth is evaluated, optimized, and aligned with a tax strategy that protects profitability, ensuring that businesses grow not just larger, but stronger, more resilient, and more valuable over time.

*"Too Big, Too Fast"*

Lena had always believed that growth was the cure for every problem, and when her software company began attracting larger clients and bigger contracts, she pushed forward relentlessly, hiring aggressively, expanding into new markets, and reinvesting every dollar she could, convinced that speed was the key to survival, until the AI system she installed revealed a future she had never considered, one where success itself became the greatest threat to her business.

The first forecast showed rapid revenue growth, exactly what Lena expected, but layered beneath it was a rising wall of tax obligations that climbed faster than cash flow, and as the AI simulated the next eighteen months, it became clear that the company would soon face overlapping payroll tax spikes, multi-state compliance requirements, and estimated payments that would arrive all at once, creating a liquidity crisis not because the company was failing, but because it was growing too fast without alignment.

At first Lena dismissed the projections, telling herself that more revenue would solve everything, but as the AI ran alternative scenarios, showing what would happen if growth continued unchecked versus what would happen if it was paced strategically, she began to see that the difference between the two futures was not ambition, but design, because in the optimized scenario the company still grew, but profits were reinvested deliberately, tax exposure was smoothed, and compliance remained manageable.

Reluctantly, Lena slowed hiring slightly, staggered market expansion, and redirected profits into qualifying investments that reduced taxable income while strengthening infrastructure, and as she watched the projections update in real time, she felt a strange mix of relief and discipline, realizing that restraint was not weakness, but strategy.

Then came the moment that proved everything, when a competitor that had grown even faster suddenly collapsed under the weight of tax penalties and cash shortages, and Lena recognized the future she had narrowly avoided, understanding that intelligence, not speed, was what separated sustainable success from spectacular failure.

As her company continued to expand, it did so with a sense of balance and control, and Lena no longer chased growth blindly, because she had learned that the goal was not to become big as quickly as possible, but to become strong enough to stay big once she arrived.

Years later, when investors praised her company's stability and profitability, Lena smiled quietly, knowing that the secret was not hidden in flashy metrics or aggressive scaling, but in the unseen discipline of aligning growth with tax intelligence, and she understood that the moment she stopped growing too fast was the moment she finally began growing right.

*Chapter 7*

# Strategic Visibility: How AI Turns Financial Blind Spots Into Competitive Advantage

Most businesses do not fail because they lack effort, intelligence, or ambition; they fail because they operate with partial visibility, making critical decisions without fully understanding how revenue, expenses, taxes, and compliance interact beneath the surface, and artificial intelligence has become the first technology capable of illuminating these hidden layers continuously, transforming blind spots into strategic insight that allows businesses to compete, grow, and optimize with clarity rather than guesswork.

Financial blind spots emerge naturally as companies scale, diversify, and accelerate, because human attention cannot track thousands of transactions, regulations, thresholds, and timing variables simultaneously, and traditional reporting systems fragment information across departments, software platforms, and advisors, leaving leaders with incomplete pictures of their true financial position, while AI unifies these signals into a single, coherent model that shows not only what is happening now but why it is happening and what it will cause next.

AI-driven visibility reveals relationships that were previously invisible, such as how marketing spend influences taxable income volatility, how payroll structure affects long-term tax efficiency, how customer concentration increases compliance risk, or how inventory decisions ripple through cash flow and depreciation schedules, and by exposing these connections, AI allows businesses to design strategies that optimize the system as a whole rather than improving one area at the expense of another.

This visibility becomes a competitive advantage because businesses that see clearly can act earlier, adjusting pricing, hiring, investment, and tax strategy before competitors recognize the same risks or opportunities, and in markets where margins are thin and compliance costs are rising, the ability to act weeks or months ahead can mean the difference between dominance and decline.

AI also enables continuous performance diagnostics, identifying inefficiencies, anomalies, and emerging risks in real time, allowing leaders to intervene before small issues compound into serious financial or tax problems, and this proactive posture replaces the reactive cycle that traps many companies in constant firefighting and penalty avoidance. As regulatory systems grow more automated and enforcement becomes more data-driven, visibility is no longer optional, because errors, inconsistencies, and inefficiencies are detected faster and punished more severely, and AI provides the only scalable way to maintain transparency, accuracy, and strategic control without overwhelming human teams.

Ultimately, AI-powered visibility transforms financial management from a rearview-mirror exercise into a forward-facing discipline where businesses operate with confidence, precision, and intent, leveraging insight as a strategic asset that compounds over time into sustained profitability and resilience.

*"The Blind Spot That Almost Cost Everything"*

When Ethan founded his logistics company, he believed that success came from speed, efficiency, and relentless execution, and for years that belief served him well as contracts grew, trucks multiplied, and revenue climbed steadily, but as the business expanded, a subtle danger formed not from missteps or recklessness, but from something far more insidious: the slow accumulation of blind spots that hid the true shape of his company beneath layers of growth.

At first, everything looked fine, because revenue reports were strong, invoices were paid, and taxes were filed on time, yet Ethan felt increasingly uneasy, as if the business was outrunning his understanding of it, because every decision seemed to create unexpected consequences somewhere else, and problems appeared suddenly without clear causes, leaving him constantly reacting instead of leading.

The moment of reckoning came when an AI-driven financial visibility system Ethan installed as an experiment produced its first comprehensive analysis, mapping cash flow, tax exposure, compliance risk, and operational dependencies into a single model, and what it revealed was not a crisis, but a pattern of hidden vulnerabilities that had quietly grown alongside the company, including overconcentration of revenue from a few clients, payroll structures that inflated tax burden, and expansion into jurisdictions that created complex compliance obligations he barely understood.

The AI showed how these blind spots interacted, demonstrating that a delay in one major client's payment could cascade into missed tax deposits, penalties, and strained vendor relationships, and for the first time Ethan saw that his company's apparent strength masked a fragility born not of weakness, but of incomplete visibility.

At first the realization was overwhelming, because fixing one issue revealed another, and each layer of insight made the system feel more complex rather than simpler, but as Ethan worked with the AI, adjusting variables and testing scenarios, clarity replaced confusion, because he began to understand not just individual problems, but the structure of the system that created them.

The AI guided him to diversify revenue timing, restructure compensation, renegotiate contracts, and simplify jurisdictional exposure, and with each change the model recalculated, showing a business that became progressively more stable, resilient, and predictable, and what surprised Ethan most was how little revenue had to change to dramatically improve outcomes once blind spots were eliminated.

Then came the real-world validation, when a major client unexpectedly paused operations, sending shockwaves through the logistics industry, and while competitors scrambled to respond, Ethan's company absorbed the impact calmly, because the risk had already been identified, modeled, and mitigated, and cash reserves, tax timing, and operational adjustments were already in place.

In the quiet weeks that followed, Ethan reflected on how close he had come to disaster without ever seeing it approach, realizing that the greatest threat to his business had never been competition or regulation, but invisibility, because what you cannot see cannot be managed, and what cannot be managed eventually controls you.

Years later, as his company became known not just for reliability but for strategic discipline, Ethan often thought back to the moment when the blind spots were first revealed, understanding that visibility was not just about data, but about power, because seeing clearly allowed him to act deliberately, grow intelligently, and lead with confidence instead of fear.

In the end, Ethan understood that intelligence did not make his business perfect or immune to risk, but it made risk visible, manageable, and survivable, and in a world where most companies stumble in the dark, that clarity became his greatest competitive advantage.

*Chapter 8*

# From Compliance to Command: How AI Turns Tax Planning Into Strategic Power

For most businesses, tax compliance has historically been viewed as a defensive obligation, something to be endured, minimized, and survived, rather than a strategic system to be mastered, yet artificial intelligence fundamentally alters this relationship by transforming tax planning from a reactive necessity into a proactive instrument of control that allows businesses not merely to comply with the rules, but to use them intelligently as part of a broader financial strategy designed to preserve capital, guide growth, and compound long-term value.

AI-driven tax command emerges when compliance data, financial forecasting, and strategic planning converge into a single intelligent framework, because taxes are not isolated events but continuous consequences of everyday decisions, and AI is uniquely capable of tracking these consequences in real time, translating complex regulations into actionable insight that empowers businesses to move deliberately rather than cautiously, with confidence instead of fear. Traditional compliance systems focus on accuracy after the fact, ensuring that filings are correct once transactions have already occurred, but AI shifts the focus forward, allowing businesses to see how future actions will affect compliance before they are taken, effectively converting tax rules into navigational markers that guide decision-making rather than obstacles that block progress.

This transition from compliance to command is critical in an era where governments increasingly rely on automated enforcement, digital reporting, and data-driven audits, because businesses that lack predictive alignment with tax systems are exposed to penalties, inefficiencies, and strategic paralysis, while those that integrate AI gain the ability to operate fluidly within regulatory boundaries without sacrificing agility or innovation.

AI also elevates the role of tax planning by embedding it directly into executive decision-making, ensuring that choices about pricing, hiring, expansion, investment, and financing are informed not only by operational considerations but by their tax implications, allowing leaders to design strategies that maximize after-tax outcomes rather than chasing pre-tax growth that erodes profitability.

As businesses grow more complex, operating across multiple jurisdictions, platforms, and revenue streams, AI becomes essential for maintaining command, because manual oversight cannot scale with complexity, and intelligent systems provide the only viable way to ensure that compliance remains seamless while strategy remains ambitious.

Ultimately, AI-driven tax command represents a shift in mindset, where taxes are no longer viewed as a cost imposed from outside, but as a variable within the business system that can be modeled, optimized, and controlled, transforming taxation from a source of stress into a source of strategic leverage.

*"The Audit That Never Came"*

For years, Michael ran his consulting firm with a quiet sense of dread that hovered in the background of every decision he made, because although the business was successful, expanding steadily across industries and borders, he knew that complexity bred risk, and somewhere beneath the layers of invoices, contracts, and filings, there was always the possibility that a mistake, oversight, or misunderstanding could trigger an audit that would unravel everything he had built.

That fear shaped how Michael operated, making him cautious to the point of restraint, avoiding bold investments, delaying expansion, and second-guessing decisions that might attract scrutiny, until the day he implemented an AI-driven tax intelligence system not out of confidence, but out of exhaustion, because he realized that living in fear of what he could not see was no way to lead a growing enterprise.

The AI's first act was not to reassure him, but to reveal how fragile his sense of compliance actually was, mapping his operations across jurisdictions, identifying inconsistencies in classification, timing mismatches in filings, and inefficiencies that increased exposure unnecessarily, and as Michael absorbed the analysis, he understood that compliance was not something he had achieved once and maintained forever, but a living condition that required continuous alignment.

What surprised him most was how the AI reframed the entire concept of compliance, showing that rules were not traps waiting to be sprung, but structures that could be navigated intelligently if understood deeply enough, and as the system simulated different decisions—new hires, pricing changes, international contracts—it showed how each move would alter his compliance posture, turning uncertainty into clarity.

Over time, Michael began to operate differently, no longer asking whether a decision might cause trouble, but how to structure it so that it fit cleanly within the rules, and that shift changed everything, because instead of shrinking his ambitions, he redesigned them, expanding into new markets with confidence, knowing that the AI had already mapped the regulatory terrain and identified the safest, most efficient paths forward.

Then came the year when audits swept through his industry, triggered by new automated enforcement systems that flagged anomalies across thousands of firms, and while competitors scrambled to assemble documents, respond to inquiries, and explain inconsistencies they had never noticed, Michael waited, watching quietly as weeks passed and no notice arrived, because his system had already aligned his filings, documentation, and financial flows with the very patterns the authorities were scanning for.

The absence of an audit felt almost surreal, because Michael had lived so long expecting one that he did not know how to process its absence, and in that quiet realization, he understood that compliance was no longer something he hoped to escape, but something he had mastered, not through perfection, but through intelligence.

As the years went on, Michael's firm grew bolder, not reckless, but deliberate, expanding strategically, investing confidently, and optimizing its structure with an ease that once seemed impossible, and he realized that the greatest gift AI had given him was not protection from audits, but freedom from fear, because when you understand the rules deeply enough to anticipate them, they lose their power to intimidate.

Looking back, Michael often reflected on how much energy he had wasted worrying about what might go wrong, and how much opportunity he had left on the table because of that fear, and he came to see that command was not about controlling authorities or outcomes, but about controlling understanding, because when you see clearly how the system works, you no longer feel trapped inside it.

In the end, the audit that never came became a symbol of something far greater, a life and a business transformed not by evasion or luck, but by clarity, foresight, and strategic alignment, proving that in the modern economy, the greatest advantage is not avoiding scrutiny, but operating so intelligently that scrutiny has nothing to find.

*Chapter 9*

# Mastering the Long Game: AI-Driven Tax Planning for Enduring Wealth

Short-term tax savings can feel like victory, but enduring wealth is built through long-term alignment, and artificial intelligence enables businesses to move beyond tactical deductions and reactive strategies into a disciplined, multi-year approach where tax planning becomes a foundational element of capital preservation, reinvestment, and compounding growth, because the most powerful financial decisions are not those that reduce taxes this quarter, but those that shape how income, assets, and obligations evolve over decades.

AI-driven long-term tax planning integrates forecasting, scenario modeling, risk analysis, and execution into a single continuous system that evaluates not just the next filing cycle, but the cumulative impact of decisions over time, allowing businesses to see how entity structure, compensation strategy, asset ownership, depreciation, reinvestment, and jurisdictional exposure interact across years to determine ultimate wealth outcomes.

This long-range perspective is critical because many tax strategies that appear beneficial in isolation can become costly when viewed over time, such as aggressive deferrals that create future spikes, structures that limit flexibility, or growth paths that trigger compounding compliance burden, and AI exposes these delayed consequences early by modeling how today's choices affect future tax rates, liquidity, exit opportunities, and valuation.

AI also enables businesses to design tax strategies that evolve as the company evolves, adjusting plans as revenue scales, markets shift, and laws change, ensuring that tax planning remains adaptive rather than rigid, and this adaptability is essential in an environment where static strategies quickly become obsolete.

One of the most valuable contributions of AI in long-term planning is its ability to align tax strategy with life-cycle goals, whether those goals involve steady cash flow, aggressive expansion, succession planning, or exit preparation, because taxes influence not just annual profit, but ownership structure, transferability, and long-term control.

As businesses move toward maturity, AI helps leaders evaluate when to optimize for income versus capital gains, when to reinvest versus distribute, and how to structure compensation and ownership to preserve wealth across generations, transforming tax planning into a tool for legacy creation rather than mere compliance.

Ultimately, AI enables businesses to master the long game by ensuring that every decision fits within a coherent, forward-looking tax strategy that compounds over time, allowing wealth to grow steadily, predictably, and sustainably.

*"The Exit That Was Designed Years Before"*

No one noticed the moment when Adrian's company became valuable, not because it happened suddenly, but because it was the result of years of quiet, deliberate decisions that never made headlines, never attracted attention, and never felt dramatic in the moment, yet when the offer finally arrived, it was clear that the outcome had been designed long before the conversation began.

Adrian had started his firm with modest ambitions, focused on stability rather than scale, but as the business grew, he noticed how easily success could be undermined by short-sighted decisions, watching peers chase immediate tax savings that later trapped them in rigid structures, forced painful restructurings, or destroyed exit value, and it was that observation—not greed or fear—that led him to adopt an AI-driven long-term tax planning system early in his journey.

The AI did not promise quick wins; instead it asked uncomfortable questions about where the business was heading, how long Adrian intended to own it, what kind of life he wanted afterward, and how much control he wished to retain, and by modeling multiple futures, it showed how choices made today would echo years later, shaping not just tax bills, but freedom, leverage, and options.

As years passed, Adrian resisted temptations that looked profitable in the short term but compromised flexibility, choosing instead to reinvest strategically, structure ownership carefully, and align compensation with long-term goals, and although some decisions appeared conservative to outsiders, the AI continuously recalculated, showing that each move increased future value while minimizing hidden liabilities.

When market conditions shifted and consolidation swept through the industry, competitors scrambled to restructure, renegotiate, and explain their financial history to potential buyers, while Adrian's company stood out for its clarity, predictability, and clean structure, because every major decision had been made with the end in mind, even when that end felt distant and abstract.

The offer arrived quietly, without urgency or pressure, because the buyer saw not just current profitability, but long-term stability and tax efficiency, and as negotiations progressed, Adrian realized that the most valuable asset he possessed was not revenue or technology, but optionality, the freedom to accept, decline, or reshape the deal on his own terms.

When the exit finally closed, the numbers confirmed what the AI had predicted years earlier: minimal tax leakage, maximum retained value, and a transition that preserved both wealth and peace of mind, and Adrian understood that the success was not the result of timing or luck, but of foresight.

In the weeks that followed, as he reflected on the journey, Adrian realized that the true benefit of long-term tax planning was not just financial, but psychological, because designing the future intentionally removed fear from the present, allowing him to lead calmly, invest wisely, and grow patiently without being distracted by short-term noise.

The exit, when it came, felt less like an ending and more like a confirmation, proof that when decisions are aligned over time, outcomes cease to be surprises and instead become the natural conclusion of a path chosen long before anyone else could see where it led.

And in that understanding, Adrian found a deeper satisfaction than any number could provide, knowing that wealth, when designed with intelligence and patience, becomes not just something you earn, but something you keep, control, and carry forward into whatever comes next.

*Chapter 10*

# The Self-Optimizing Business: How AI Creates Permanent Tax Intelligence

The final evolution of AI-driven financial forecasting and tax planning is not prediction, automation, or even optimization, but self-correction, because the most advanced businesses do not merely follow strategies; they continuously refine them, adapting automatically as conditions change, and artificial intelligence enables this by creating systems that learn from outcomes, detect inefficiencies, and improve decision-making over time, transforming tax planning from a manual discipline into a living, self-optimizing intelligence embedded within the business itself.

A self-optimizing business uses AI to observe how forecasts compare to reality, identifying gaps between projected and actual results, and adjusting future models accordingly, ensuring that predictions grow more accurate and strategies more refined with each cycle, and this feedback loop is essential because no forecast is ever perfect, yet a system that learns from its errors becomes more powerful over timc than one that simply follows static rules. In the context of tax planning, this means that AI does not merely calculate liabilities, but studies how deductions perform, how timing strategies affect liquidity, how compliance patterns influence audit risk, and how growth decisions impact long-term tax efficiency, allowing it to recommend increasingly precise actions that align profitability, compliance, and sustainability.

This permanent intelligence allows businesses to move beyond reliance on annual planning sessions or quarterly reviews, instead operating in a continuous state of awareness where every transaction subtly improves the system's understanding of the business, and over time this compounding insight becomes one of the most valuable assets a company possesses, because it embeds institutional knowledge directly into its operations.

As governments adopt AI-driven enforcement, real-time reporting, and automated compliance, businesses that lack self-optimizing systems will fall behind, not because they are reckless, but because they cannot adapt fast enough, while those that embrace intelligent feedback loops will remain aligned, efficient, and resilient even as rules evolve.

The self-optimizing business does not eliminate human judgment; it elevates it, freeing leaders from reactive decision-making and allowing them to focus on vision, ethics, and strategy while AI handles the complexity of execution, ensuring that tax planning remains precise, compliant, and aligned with long-term goals.

In this final chapter, the series culminates in a vision of the business not as a static entity that reacts to taxes, but as an intelligent system that continuously learns how to earn, protect, and compound wealth with minimal friction, preparing the reader for the broader future of AI-powered taxation explored in the final volume of this professional series.

*"The Business That Learned"*

When Evelyn looked back over twenty years of entrepreneurship, she realized that the most exhausting part of running a business had never been the work itself, but the constant uncertainty, the feeling that no matter how careful she was, something unexpected could undo years of effort, and although technology had improved speed and efficiency, it had never truly removed that uncertainty until the moment her company crossed an invisible threshold and became something fundamentally different: a business that learned.

It began quietly, with an AI system designed to forecast taxes and cash flow, but over time Evelyn noticed that the system was no longer merely responding to inputs, but adapting, adjusting projections based on past outcomes, flagging patterns she had missed, and refining its recommendations with a subtlety that felt almost intuitive, and she realized that the company was no longer relying on static strategy, but on a form of intelligence that evolved alongside it.

At first, the learning process revealed uncomfortable truths, showing that some strategies she had trusted for years were less effective than she believed, and that certain habits, though familiar, created unnecessary tax friction, yet instead of forcing abrupt change, the AI introduced gradual improvements, testing alternatives, measuring results, and refining its guidance until efficiency improved without disruption.

Year after year, the system became sharper, predicting tax liabilities with uncanny accuracy, identifying opportunities earlier, and smoothing cash flow so effectively that financial stress became rare, and Evelyn found herself making decisions with a confidence she had never known, because outcomes were no longer guesses, but well-understood consequences of intelligently modeled choices.

The most profound moment came during an economic downturn, when uncertainty spread across her industry, and while competitors scrambled to react, cutting staff and freezing investment, Evelyn's company adjusted calmly, because the AI had already learned how the business behaved under stress, had already optimized reserves, timing, and compliance, and had already prepared a path forward. As the economy recovered, her business emerged stronger, not because it had avoided difficulty, but because it had learned from every previous challenge, embedding resilience into its very structure, and Evelyn understood that intelligence was no longer something external she consulted, but something internal that shaped the business continuously.

Years later, as she prepared to step back from daily operations, Evelyn realized that her greatest achievement was not revenue, market share, or even profit, but continuity, because the business could now adapt without her, guided by systems that embodied years of experience, judgment, and learning, ensuring that the intelligence she had built would endure.

In that realization, Evelyn found peace, knowing that she had not merely built a company, but had designed a living system capable of sustaining itself intelligently through whatever future awaited, and she understood that true success was not found in predicting the future once, but in creating something that could learn its way through it forever.

And as she closed her laptop one evening, watching the system quietly recalibrate forecasts for the months ahead, Evelyn smiled, knowing that the uncertainty she once feared had been replaced by something far more powerful than control: understanding, continuously growing, endlessly refining, and always prepared.

# Final Thoughts

*Engineering Financial Intelligence for the Long Term*

The purpose of this book has never been to teach businesses how to chase tax savings in isolated moments, but to show how artificial intelligence allows financial clarity, forecasting accuracy, and tax control to merge into a single strategic system that operates continuously, intelligently, and with long-term intent, because the true cost of taxes is rarely the amount paid, but the uncertainty, inefficiency, and missed opportunity created by operating without foresight.

Across every chapter, one reality has become clear: businesses do not lose money because taxes exist, they lose money because taxes arrive faster than understanding, faster than preparation, and faster than liquidity, and AI fundamentally changes this equation by giving leaders visibility into the future before it becomes unavoidable, turning financial consequences into manageable variables rather than disruptive surprises.

When forecasting becomes predictive instead of reactive, cash flow stops being fragile and begins to stabilize; when scenario modeling becomes habitual, risk shifts from something feared to something engineered; and when execution is guided by intelligent systems, tax planning evolves from an annual scramble into a permanent operating advantage that compounds quietly over time.

Artificial intelligence does not remove responsibility from business owners or replace professional judgment; instead, it amplifies both by exposing patterns humans cannot see consistently, by tracking complexity humans cannot manage manually, and by creating feedback loops that allow strategy to improve with each cycle, ensuring that financial intelligence deepens rather than decays as a business grows.

One of the most powerful realizations enabled by AI-driven forecasting is that financial success is not linear, because small decisions made consistently can outperform dramatic moves made occasionally, and AI excels precisely because it optimizes the small, cumulative choices that shape tax outcomes, liquidity, resilience, and valuation across months, years, and decades.

This book has shown that compliance is no longer the ceiling of financial responsibility, but the floor, and that businesses capable of commanding their financial systems—rather than merely complying with them—operate with confidence, speed, and freedom that others struggle to attain, not because they take more risk, but because they understand risk deeply enough to manage it intelligently.

As regulatory environments grow more automated and enforcement becomes more data-driven, businesses that lack predictive alignment will increasingly pay more, not due to wrongdoing, but due to inefficiency, while those who embed AI-driven intelligence into their operations will find themselves operating smoothly within the system rather than constantly reacting to it.

Perhaps the most important outcome of adopting AI financial forecasting and tax planning is peace of mind, because when leaders know their future obligations, understand their long-term trajectory, and see the consequences of decisions before making them, anxiety gives way to clarity, and clarity becomes the foundation for confident growth.

This book represents the final step before entering a fully automated tax future, where financial systems learn, adapt, and self-correct continuously, and the businesses that embrace this evolution early will not only retain more profit, but build organizations that endure volatility, scale without penalty, and transition ownership or leadership without chaos.

As you close this volume, the goal is not for you to memorize tools or tactics, but to adopt a new mindset: one where financial intelligence is continuous, tax strategy is intentional, and artificial intelligence becomes the silent partner that ensures every dollar earned serves a purpose beyond the present moment.